Granny's Camera

By
Charron M. Mollette

Table of Contents

Dedication Page

To my great-grandmother Stella Louise Pettus and her 1940's Kodak Brownie Reflex camera.

Preface

This book was written to pay homage to my great-grandmother Stella Louise Pettus and her 1940's Kodak Brownie Reflex camera.

Introduction

Have you ever looked at a photograph and thought about the moment it was taken?
"Click!"
Time stands still.

Chapter 1 "Granny"

One rainy afternoon in October, I was unpacking Halloween decorations from my closet, when I came across a box of family photos. I was drawn to this particular portrait of my great-grandmother, Stella Louise Pettus.

Stella Louise Pettus was born on October 11th 1904 in Gurdon, AR to the late William and Anna Berry. She attended school in Arkadelphia and Little Rock, AR.

In 1943 she lived in Port Orchard, WA along with her brother Robert Berry (pictured above), husband, and children. Years later moving to Seattle, WA.

Left to right: Ella Havland, Stella Pettus, Annie Stirgus, Myrtle Francois [housekeeper], Jimmie Wayne, Vallie Jefferson.

She retired from University Properties Janitorial Services after 12 years.

Granny always wore her "Sunday Blessed". She faithfully attended Mount Zion Baptist Church and was a member of "The Rebecca Circle Missionary Society".

I remember one Easter, as she pinned her bonnet in place, she jokingly said, "Pray with me, but don't Play with me." (pictured below: Granny's stunt double)

10

This is the star, Granny's 1940's Kodak Brownie Reflex camera, with it she captured many special moments and events.

Granny always took my picture on the first day of school.

Sept 6, 1978   Charron 5th

After school, a certain 5th grader would walk to her great-grandmother's cozy, 3rd floor apartment. She'd be greeted with warm hugs as Aretha Franklin played on the living room stereo.

After completing her homework, at the dining room table, she'd read poems from her favorite book, "Where the Sidewalk Ends".

The two would then talk about their day over an early supper of Salmon Croquettes, "La specialite de la maison" (The specialty of the house).

"Croquettes & Cornbread"

When I was young, I'd help Granny,
in the Kitchen we'd be...
Boiling Mustard and Collard Greens,
Watching "Soap Operas" on T.V.

Catfish from "Pike Place Market",
Cornmeal, Pepper and Salt...
It's "Aretha Franklin" good,
Exceptional. Kept in a Vault.

In Every room, the Delicious aroma,
of Ox Tails or Neck Bones...
Counting my Blessings, Every day,
as Precious Diamond Stones.

Feeding the Soul. A Fairytale.
Like a Castle, with a Drawbridge...
What Recipe has captured my Heart?
This Late-Night Snack, from the Fridge.

At Night, I'd Thank the Heavens,
before resting my Sleepy Head...
For Faith, Family, Granny's Camera,
Salmon Croquettes and Cornbread.

When I was young, I'd help Granny,
in the Kitchen, we'd be...
Boiling Mustard and Collard Greens,
Watching "Soap Operas" on T.V.

Granny taught Mom and I how to crochet (a French term meaning 'small hook'). She created colorful "granny square" afghans by interlocking loops of yarn. Some say, "Crocheting is like knitting, but it's knot".

It took 6 hours and 17 minutes for our flight to Maui. It was so hot and humid that when I saw the Heat wave, I waved back. *("ba-dum-TSH!")*

Aunt Jimmie's homemade ice cream was the highlight of our 4th of July barbecues. Churned on the back porch in a wooden bucket, its ingredients consisted of sugar, vanilla, cream, ice, and rock salt.

Black Diamond's blue skies and four generations of women captured on film.

1978

Me, Granny, and Gram on Thanksgiving Day
(1978). The sounds of football watchers "Booing" could
be heard from the den. The aroma of turkey, dressing,
macaroni and cheese, yams, mustard greens, and pecan
pie filled the house as family and friends arrived.

I remember Saturday mornings. Granny eating her grits and eggs, while I devoured a bowl of Frosted Flakes watching "Popeye" cartoons.

Our Saturday routine: a bus ride downtown and lunch at Woolworth's. We sat on chrome, "Soda Fountain" swivel stools. Even though my feet didn't reach the floor, I was just tall enough to see the top of a puffy, white hat in the kitchen. As I slurped my chocolate milkshake, the waitress belted out our order like a spirited hymn: *"Two Burrr-ger Plat-ters!"*

Dadda' Reese was distinguished in his double-breasted suits. They were reminiscent of the costume designs for the 1934 film "The Thin Man". Granny's contagious laugh made her a motion picture "Starlet".

Sinatra songs echoed in my head every time I saw them together. After years of courtship, they married, then eventually moved to Washington State from Arkansas.

They were the essence of elegance and sophistication whenever they attended church or formal gatherings.

Dadda' Reese was debonair and handsome in his "Madison Cap-Toe" Stacy Adams and "Boater" straw hat. His cigars were always carefully tucked away in his shirt pocket.

"Dadda' Reese"

He Represents, the School of "Hard Knocks"...
He's "Richard Pryor". He's Rare Diamond Rocks.

Horse-racing at "Long-acres", winning a bet...
Rectangle Riches, from Sunrise to Sunset.

Reporters. Rave Reviews. His Gentleman Style...
A Mount Rainier Mansion. A Relaxing Smile.

He Reflects. He Reads. His "Skillz", are no Joke...
He's Barbecue Ribs. He's Cigar Smoke.

A Routine Reminder, I should mention...
His "Stacey Adams", cause "Hater Conventions".

Faithfully Righteous, it's no Surprise...
Smooth like Peanut Butter, or Ketchup on Fries.

Repeat this Recipe, His Heart is for Real...
He's "Redd Foxx", hosting "Let's Make a Deal".

Rebellious. Rhythmic. Kind-Hearted and Good...
He's Dadda' Reese. A Modern day "Robin Hood".

Their union brought forth two daughters, Ann Marie and Charlotte Louise.

My grandmother, Ann Marie Pettus (a.k.a. "Gram"), was born on November 14th 1928 in Little Rock, AR.

She had the figure of Dorothy Dandridge, the charisma of Eartha Kitt, and loved the music of Nancy Wilson.

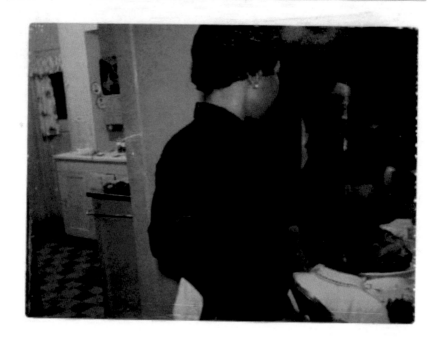

She was a pastor's wife and a mother. Gifted in the kitchen, she hardly ever used measuring cups or spoons when she cooked or baked. As she prepared meals, music would play on the living room record player. The family favorites were her signature "Lemon Icebox" and Pecan Pies.

"Lemon Icebox Pie"

A box of "Nilla" wafer cookies. Butter, half a stick...
A teaspoon of vanilla. Two lemons, do the trick.

One can of milk, "Eagle Brand". Add whipped cream...
Sweetness from the icebox. A dessert-lovers dream.

In a glass pie pan, crush cookies, into melted butter...
Line pan with cookies, this treat, will make you
stut-ter.

In a bowl, mix "Eagle Brand", and lemon juice...
Add vanilla extract, giving it a boost.

Pour mixture into pan. Let it chill overnight...
From fridge to plate, we could hardly wait,
for Gram's "Lemon Icebox Delight".

Our Annual Walker Chapel A.M.E. Church Barbecues helped build our congregation and strengthened our community. I learned how to Give from the Heart, "Bee" kind, and to Always have Faith.

"Ann Marie"

She's Awesome. She's Autumn. She's April
Afternoons...
Loves her Purple Bathroom. She's A Bouquet of
Balloons.

In Addition to Algebra, She's Truly Upper Class...
Analyzes Everything, with Wit And Sass.

The Academy Awards, gave her Applause...
Signing Autographs. She winked, just because.

She's like An Attorney, make no mistake...
She's Adjectives And Adverbs. She's 7-UP Cake.

Driving A yellow Cadillac, to the market for food...
Shopping Boutiques, for some "Diva Bad-di-tude".

According to her Agent, She's modeling in Paris...
Rumored She's Royalty, And may be An Heiress.

The sounds of Nancy Wilson, fill Every Room...
Soap Operas. Sardines. Ritz crackers. Vacuum.

The Answer is clear. The reason why...
"Gram" is the Queen of, "Lemon Icebox Pie".

On our trip to the Far East, Gram, Mom, and I toured downtown Hong Kong by way of water taxi, more commonly known as a "Junkyard" boat. (The captain was kind enough to take this picture)

We enjoyed local cuisine, gazed at historic sight-seeing spots, and shopped along the downtown streets. We landed into Sea-Tac Airport, our bulging suitcases stuffed with memorable souvenirs.

Her bathroom was purple, the color of royalty.
Purple walls. Purple rugs. Purple Bath towels. Purple
guest towels. Purple.
She loved it. And so did we. She kept it neat and clean.
And so did we.
It was because of her tidiness that she was nicknamed
"The Warden" by Uncle Gordon.

My great Aunt, Charlotte Louise Pettus (a.k.a. "Aunt Chockey"), was born on June 5th 1931 in Arkadelphia, AR. She moved to Port Orchard, WA in 1943 with her family and was a proud graduate of Garfield High School.

She joined Mount Zion Baptist Church where she sang
in the Junior Choir and became a member of the Puget
Sound Missionary Usher Board.

"Aunt Chockey"

She's Cute. Creative. Charlotte's her name...
She's "Coco Chanel". Legendary Fame.

She Cuddles her Kids. She makes Birthday Cakes...
Her Smile Shines Bright. She's Angelic Snowflakes.

The Curious were Caught, Copying her Clothes...
She's the Joy of Spring. The Beauty of a Rose.

She's Charming. Adorable. Kicks Clowns to the Curb...
Criss-Crossing Constantly, her Nouns and Verbs.

Her Heart, Soft as Cashmere. Culinary-Clever...
She's my Inspiration. I'll Love Her Forever.

She's Sweet Potato Pie. Chocolate Chip Ice Cream...
A Sister. A Mother. The Aunt of my Dreams.

She's Cute. Creative. Charlotte's her name...
She's "Coco Chanel". Legendary Fame.

37

My whimsical cousin, Darrel Eugene Franklin (pictured with Granny), was born on October 6th 1957 to Uncle Floyd and Charlotte Louise Franklin.

The oldest of two children, he was involved in C.A.Y.A. (Central Area Youth Association). He played various activities such as Little League Football, Track and Field, Ski School, "Young Life" Cub Scouts, and later becoming a member of the NAACP.

He attended Stevens Elementary, Meany Jr. High School, John Marshall, Roosevelt High School, and was a proud graduate of Garfield High School (Class of '76). He also attended Shoreline Community College and was a very dedicated employee of "The Associated Recreational Council" as a Child Care Counselor for the City of Seattle. He joined the Junior choir and became an usher at Mount Zion Baptist Church.

"Darrel"

He's a Duet of Drums. He's the Dawn of a New Day...
His Dazzling Smile, are the writings of Hemingway.

A "Garfield Bulldog". A Coach on the scene...
A Fun-loving Prankster. Darrel Eugene.

Dominating Debates, Diplomats know his name...
He's Three-Dimensional, like the Dominoes Game.

A Decimal Dynamo, always Doubling his Dollars...
Determined Drive. Fierce in his "Dawg" collar.

Without Delay to Dallas, then a Detroit Dash...
Then a Pitstop to Denmark, turning Dividends to Cash.

He's the Dime, in this Rhyme. The Perfect Ten...
He's "Dy-No-Mite!", signing Autographs in Pen.

A Debonair Dude. Never met a stranger...
Douses Dragons. Laughs at Danger.

Devoted to Loved Ones, in our Family Tree...
He's "Funkin' for Jamaica". He's part of me.

He's a Duet of Drums. He's the Dawn of a New Day...
His Dazzling Smile, are the writings of Hemingway.

41

My sweet cousin, Shawn Louise Franklin, was born on December 14th 1960 to Uncle Floyd and Charlotte Louise Franklin. (pictured: Aunt Chockey holding Shawn, Mom, and older brother Darrel Eugene at Gram's house)

Darrel and Shawn.

Cousin Shawn at Granny's.

"Shawn"

It's no Secret She Shines, like the Stars in the Sky...
She's Sunshine. She's Saturdays without having to try.

Steppin' with her Drill Team. Marching in a Parade...
A "Jack and Jill" Debutante. Her Gown, custom made.

On September Sixteenth, She's Scheduled to Speak...
Her Secretary Says She's busy, the next Several weeks.

Spotted on Safari, from Sweden to Spain...
Taking a Six-minute Snooze, on Seattle's Dinner Train.

If She ran for State Senate, She'd be a Shoe-in...
Silly Slickers try to Swindle. They never win.

A Supper of Spinach Salad, at a Sushi Cafe...
May Splurge on Strawberries, on warm Sunny Days.

A Social Scholar, Sharing Truth in your ear...
Smooth as Stevie Wonder, Singing Shakespeare.

Her Spectacuar Smile, indeed Hugs my Heart...
Stylish Sunshades. She Scribbles Works of Art.

It's no Secret She Shines, like the Stars in the Sky...
She's Sunshine. She's Saturdays without having to try.

Pictured above from l to r: Darrel, Shawn, me, and Aunt Chockey; below from l to r: Darrel, Mom, me, and Shawn.

Pictured above: Shawn, Granny, Darrel, me, and Auntie
Bug; below: Darrel and Shawn celebrating my birthday.

Shawn was a member of the high-stepping Majorettes Drill Team. Her tasseled boots had metal taps on the heels and outsoles. They made a cool *"Clickety-click"* sound when she marched with her dance troupe.

Shawn and Darrel, two names that became one
magical word, "Shawn-Darrel".
We would play games like "Hide-N-Seek" outside of
Granny's house. It was a wonderland for our
imaginations, amusement, and mischievous moments.

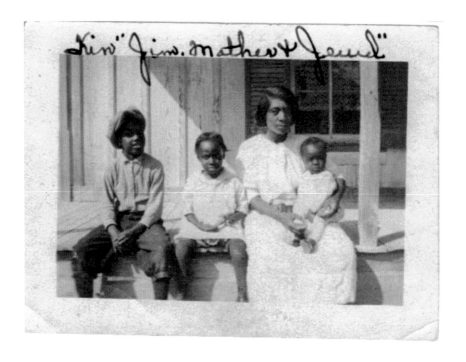

My grandfather, Jewel Bryson DeWitty (a.k.a. "Poppee"), was born on January 12th 1924 in Austin, TX to parents Neal and Josephine DeWitty. (pictured above from l to r: a cousin, my great Aunt Jimmie, great-grandmother Josephine and Poppee)

After graduating high school, he enlisted into the United States Navy serving in World War II.

The Lord called him to serve in the church. He was ordained an Itinerant Elder for the Puget Sound Conference at Bailey African Methodist Church in Everett, WA from 1957-59. He was then assigned as Pastor of Walker Chapel A.M.E. Church in Seattle, WA (pictured below) and served for 16 years. The membership grew from a total of 20 in 1959 to 122 by 1972. He attended his first conference in 1960.

He was then promoted to Presiding Elder of the A.M.E. church's Puget Sound Conference. He had many years of spiritual training under the guidance of the late Presiding Elder Lawrence Fisher Greene, who retired in 1975.

Poppee's tactics when playing dominoes were strategic, calculating, and swift. It was nicknamed "bones" because the rectangular tiles were made from either wood or ivory.

Poppee, me, and Gram.

"Sunday School"

Harmonizing Hymns. Prayers from Above...
Sunday School. Choir Singing. Kindness and Love.

Pursue your Purpose. Respect is Earned...
Thankful and Grateful, for the Lessons I've Learned.

Baptism. Communion. A Journey from the Start...
Gifts of Love. Giving from the Heart.

Mahalia Jackson singing, "In the Upper Room"...
Aretha "Says a Little Prayer", with Poetic Bloom.

"Until I Found The Lord". Yes, He Loves me...
A Growing Congregation. Our Family Tree.

"The Word" has Strength. The Power It has...
It's Uplifting Laughter. It's Groovy Jazz.

Dreams dancing Gracefully. Destiny takes Flight...
I Believe in Its Rhythm. In Its Rhythm I Write.

Studying Scripture. Each Verse is rehearsed...
It's Meaningful Poetry. It's putting Faith First.

Students are Inspired, as Poppee Teaches...
Singing his Sermons. He Listens. He Preaches.

Harmonizing Hymns. Prayers from Above...
Sunday School. Choir Singing. Kindness and Love.

Poppee preparing his sermon for Sunday morning church service.

Pictured above: Poppee and Mom; below: former President Jimmy Carter and Poppee.

Chapter 7 "The Rev. and The Warden"

My mom's parents were a remarkable couple. Two hardworking, loving individuals...

with a silly side.

They met, married, and after some time, moved into a quaint house on the corner of 24th and Roy St. in Seattle, WA.

The house vibrated with the sounds of Al Green, Mahalia Jackson, The Temptations, Nancy Wilson and more. The pink kitchen's windows would be steamed up from Sunday's dinner which consisted of beef roast, mashed potatoes, corn bread, and on other occasions, Chitlin's and Collard Greens.

Gram and Poppee had four children, Ann (my mother) the oldest; the second daughter Myra was out of camera range; the youngest daughter Lawana; and Gordon.

Uncle Gordon, Mom, and Auntie Bug at our "DeWitty Family Reunion" in Sparks, NV (1997).

My mom, Ann Ruthera DeWitty, was born on November 9th 1946 in Tacoma, WA.

She was a member of "The Girl Scouts of America" and a Garfield High School graduate.

Mom age 12 (1959)

She worked for United Airlines as a reservationist for over 30 years. A natural born leader with a loving heart.

(Photo taken by Yuen Lui Photography Studios)

"Cool Water"

The Essence of Cool Water, She's November Snow...
Intriguing. Ambitious, with Poetic Flow.

Protects her Loved Ones, A Leader on duty...
As the Ocean surrounds, Hawaiian Beauty.

Water-falling Wisdom, A "Whodunit" seeker...
"The Coolest Mom Ever", in "Converse" sneakers.

Brilliant. Brave. Raindrops in Springtime...
A Genius at Math. "The Wiz" of this Rhyme.

When rippling Floods Rise, from All directions...
She Stays Afloat, Bridging connections.

She's White River Rafting, in Stormy Seas...
Her Words are soothing, like a hot cup of Tea.

A Daughter, A Sister. An Aunt. A Mother...
A Girl Scout. A Bulldog. A Woman like No other.

A Scorpion. A "Seahawk", from the Emerald City...
Her Softball teammates, call her "DeWitty".

The Essence of Cool Water, She's November Snow...
Intriguing. Ambitious, with Poetic Flow.

In 1970, Mom and I moved into this two-bedroom house on the corner of 27th and Howell in the Central area of Seattle. It gained a reputation from visitors for its frightfully intimidating staircase. The first set of steps were made of cement with green ivy growing through cracks of a wall on the right side. After a mid-climb landing, the second set of steps were made of creaking wood leading up to the front door. I didn't have a snowball's chance of sneaking in or out after curfew.

Granny and her trusty photog skills documented Mom's first car, a 1965 Volkswagen Beetle.

Mom and I on our vacation to the mystical island of O'ahu. We enjoyed swaying palm trees, the bluest skies, chocolate-covered macadamia nuts, pineapple flavored "Crush" soda pop, and snorkeling.

"Bird Seed"

I know a Parrot named "Sunny". Beautiful and Nice...
Playful as Penguin, Speed-skating on Ice.

Candy Coated Rainbows, a Cockatiel called "Skittles"...
She's Regal as an Eagle, munching on her vittles.

Jokester. Jester. "Billy Jack". Cooing before Dawn...
Once Upon An Ugly Duckling, who turned into a Swan.

I Danced to "Flock of Seagulls", in Nineteen Eighty-Two...
No Vulture Vibes, at the "Flamingo", with its Penthouse view.

In Bodega Bay, a Hitchcock Thriller, if you haven't heard...
I Learned about "Sesame Street", from a Yellow Bird.

Daffy and Donald Duck, playing Chess and Checkers...
Woody parties, with his "Homies", Hawks and Woodpeckers.

Road Runner outwits every time. Daisy Duck, a Sweetie...
"I Tawt I Taw a Puddy Tat." A clever quote from Tweety.

A Blue Jays player, Pigeon-toed, pitching on the mound...
Peacocks peek at Zookeepers, throwing insects on the ground.

I go Crazy for Cuckoo Clocks, an automated Fowl...
Time for a Wise, Hooting Owl, already on the Prowl.

Gobble, Gobble. Feast your eyes. Did the Chicken cross the road?
A Cardinal Fact, you'll never "Quack", this Canary Code.

Mom (pictured below) was a member of the United Airlines Seattle Softball team. After retiring, she joined the Mercer Island Rockers Senior Softball League, where her clutch hit brought in the winning run for the Championship.

Like mother, like daughter. I also played softball for Holy Names Academy (Class of '86).

Me and Mom in Sparks, NV for the DeWitty Family Reunion (1997).

Dear Mom,

   You are the reason I became a writer. You taught me Love, Integrity, Kindness, and Compassion. Thank you for staying up until midnight helping me study for my 7th grade history test. I got a 91%.
I'm truly Blessed to have you as my mom. I Love you with All my heart.

Chapter 9 "The General"

My Uncle, Gordon Berry DeWitty, was born on June 24th 1949 with an eye condition called "glaucoma". A disease that is caused by fluid pressure to the optic nerve. It may have taken his sight, but it never blinded his vision.

Poppee, Uncle Gordon, and Gram.

He was best known for playing the piano. However, his favorite keyboard instrument was the "B-3 organ". At the age of 12 he became "The World's Youngest Disc Jockey" at Radio Station "K-ZAM" 92.5 FM in Seattle. (pictured below upper left)

He was inspired to move to Los Angeles to pursue his music career. (Larry, Mom, and Uncle Gordon)

Pictured above: Uncle Gordon with Sly of "Sly and the Family Stone"; below: Me with "Bloodstone" member and songwriter Mr. Charles McCormick in 1973.

"Piano Man"

A Piano Poet was born. A True Visionary...
A Story about my Uncle, Mister Gordon Berry.

He's Bad like "Shaft". Curtis Mayfield, "Super Fly"...
His Witty Words of Wisdom, Stump and Mystify.

A Gifted Disc Jockey, at a Seattle Radio Station...
He's Music Notes, Funny Quotes, in my Imagination.

He's a Jazzy General. He's the Beat of the Night...
He's Reflections of Rhythm. Harmony takes Flight.

Practice. Practice. Practice. Gold Record Beats...
"Green Apple" is the vibe. "Life in the Big City" Streets.

His Billy Dee Smile, Tickles the Happy in me...
He's Show. He's Business. Flourishing the Family Tree.

From Waves to Afro. From Dreadlocks to Grey...
His private portfolio, a Tropical Getaway.

Serenading me to sleep, with a sweet lullaby...
Mr. "Forty-Four" graduated, from Queen Anne High.

A Piano Poet was born. A True Visionary...
That's the Story of my Uncle, Mister Gordon Berry.

He became a member of Bobby Womack's band landing him record deals, performing with talented artists such as Bloodstone; Delaney and Bonnie; Earth, Wind, and Fire; Johnny Nash; Lowell George and Little Feet; Sly and the Family Stone; Bill Withers; and Charles Wright and the Watts 103rd Street Rhythm Band.

He was also an accomplished song writer, co-producer, and composer, working on such tracks as "Everybody has an Aura" performed by Chaka Khan; "You Give Me Good Vibration" performed by Johnny Nash; Con Funk Shun's "To the Max" album and "If You Don't Want My Love" which he co-wrote with Bobby Womack. His hard work earned him three Gold Records.

After a long music career, he became a keynote speaker and consultant for "Disabilities Awareness". He then founded a consulting company called "Abilities 2020". He once told me, "Music is Life, that's why the heart beats."

Lawana Reese DeWitty, the youngest of four children, was born on July 23rd 1951. A proud graduate of Garfield High School and The University of Washington. She earned her teaching credentials at UCLA and taught in Compton, CA.

Graduation day for Auntie Bug from the University of Washington (1973).

Me and Auntie Bug getting caught sneaking around Gram's kitchen for snacks (Christmas 1984).

"An Apple for Teacher"

She's a Garfield Bulldog. An Academic Scholar...
Proud in her Cap and Gown, with a purple collar.

A College Student studying, to become a Teacher "Sub"...
Got her Masters at UCLA, was a "Dawg" at "U-DUB".

Reading. Grading papers. An Art Gallery Nerd...
Taught me to embrace my gift. She is "Spoken Word".

Summer visits. A "Famous" cookie. "Amos" is the name...
Disneyland. Venice Beach. Hollywood's Walk of Fame.

She's Stevie Wonder's album, "Hotter Than July"...
She's Judith Jamison performing, in Alvin Ailey's "Cry".

She's Compton, California and the streets of East L.A.
A Daughter. A Sister. A Mother. An essay.

An Apple for the Teacher. For my Auntie Bug...
She's a Lovable Leo, wrapped in a Hug.

She's a Garfield Bulldog. An Academic Scholar...
Proud in her Cap and Gown, with a purple collar.

ARRIVALS

DEPARTURES

9-1-91

My adorable cousin Charlotte Estell Smith, Auntie Bug's only daughter, was born on April 8th 1987. A proud graduate of Franklin High School. She attended college in Nevada with a major in Political Science and Theater. She later earned a Cosmetology degree. Thanks to the learned crochet skills of her Auntie Ann, passed down from Granny, she learned how to crochet and cook. (pictured above: Charlotte greeting me at Sea-Tac Airport arriving from Philadelphia, PA).

"Charlotte"

She's Smooth, on the move, like a Porsche at top speed...
Possessing the Finesse of a Lady. Indeed.

She's Precise. Triple Nice. She's Sugar and Spice...
The Paparazzi follow her. The Diva of Diamond Ice.

She's a Chef in the Kitchen. She goes Crochet Crazeee...
Her Hubby King says, She is the "Queen Bee".

She's Hip-Hop, like Snoop Dogg. She's Fortune and
Fame...
She's my Beautiful cousin, and "Charlotte" is her name.

The most romantic proposal I ever heard was the one from Mr. Rashad Nickles to my cousin Charlotte, "I can't be your boyfriend anymore". He then presented her with an engagement ring.

"The Nickles"

Like a Beautiful Fairytale, a Love Story began...
Besties. Homies. When Harlequin met Spiderman.

A Magical Carpet Ride, from Friends to Courtship...
Became a Dynamic Duo, of Gladys Knight and one "Pip".

The Ring? Purple "Bling". His Queen. Her King...
Poetic as "The Isley Brothers", and every song they sing.

They're Love and Hip Hop. They're Girl and Boy...
They're Bride and Groom, sharing tears of Joy.

It's Soft Drinks and Donuts, for the Mister and Mrs.
A Toast to the Couple, along with Best Wishes.

New House. New Home. A Cozy Fireplace...
Memories and Mementos, adorn their Stylish Bookcase.

Painting Party Part One. Quiet and Quaint...
Part Two. Hair and Clothes covered in Paint.

Moving Day, Grooving Day. Upstairs and Down...
We hauled the "U-Haul", with the Keepsake Wedding
Gown.

Boxes upon Boxes, and More Boxes Galore...
"Ding-dong! Knock, knock". Guests arrive at the door.

A Celebration. A Blessing. My Heart they Tickles...
A New Journey Beginning, for The Newlywed Nickles.

My grandfather, Clifford R. Mollette, was one of eight children born circa 1920 in Beaumont, TX. Granny loved fixing his favorite dishes like Gumbo with crab legs and Okra, or Ox Tails with red beans, rice, and cornbread.

Three generations of Mollettes. Grandpa Clifford, Dad, and me.

Dad, older sister Beverly (a.k.a. "Auntie Bev"), and
Grandpa Clifford.

"Beaumont, Texas"

Sittin' on a Porch Swing, watchin' Grass Grow...
No Worries. No Hurries. Laid back. Nice n' Slow.

Humid. Hot. Clothes stickin' to my skin...
Sweat frames my face, creepin' down my chin.

Train Tracks, Dirt roads, Wide Country Blocks...
Crawfishin' spots, for skippin' flat Rocks.

Crickets gossipin', from Mornin' 'til Night...
Fly swatters, no match, for Mosquitos that bite.

Church-goin' folks. Rejoicin'. Bibles clutched...
Swayin' in the Spirit, by Him I've been touched.

Wise women knittin', with Bi-focal glasses...
Deep-fried Okra. Gumbo. Molasses.

Cousins upon cousins, I didn't know I had...
Southern Hospitality, Ain't too bad.

Sittin' on a Porch Swing, watchin' Grass Grow...
No Worries. No Hurries. Laid back. Nice n' Slow.

My father, Clifford R. Mollette Jr., was born on September 6th 1943 in Beaumont, TX. The son of Clifford R. Mollette and Lola Mae Carter. The Man, The Myth, The Legend worked for the Seattle Fire Department for over 26 years. Granny was tickled to pieces whenever she saw or took pictures of this "Dad-Daughter Duo".

This picture is one of my absolute favorites, Clam
digging with Mom and Dad.

Dear Dad,

Thank you for your charming wit, giving spirit, and teaching me how to put snow chains on. I Love you very much. (pictured: Me, Dad, and Mom fishing in Oregon)

"Dad"

He's unlike any other. He's scenes from "Paper Moon"...
A Father-Daughter Duo. Comedians. A Cartoon.

A Brave, young Army Soldier. The Motown Generation...
He's Witty and Captivating, with his Verbal Illustration.

"The Four Tops" is my Pops. From my high chair...
I'd "Reach Out", and he'd Always be there.

A Firefighter. A Trailblazer. Tomorrows will come...
Yesterdays and Todays, become as One.

The First Day of School. Proud moments Indeed...
Learned to Read and Write. Learned to Write and Read.

Father-Daughter Dances, in his Formal Attire...
A "James Brown Gentleman". His Courage, I Admire.

Wearing my Cap and Gown. Graduation. Adulthood...
The Beaumont Family Tree, clapping as they stood.

Road Trip to Mexico. Fished Crappie. On the Coast...
"Fue un Gran Dia", that's what I remember the most.

Classic Cars with a Clutch, was my Driver's Ed...
Thanking the Lord for my Dad, before going to Bed.

He's unlike any other. He's scenes from "Paper Moon"...
A Father-Daughter Duo. Comedians. A Cartoon.

During the late 1940's, downtown street photographers took spontaneous pictures of unsuspecting shoppers. (pictured from l to r: my great Aunt Jimmie; her only daughter Josephine, age 5; and Gram, in Tacoma, WA)

My great Aunt Jimmie Ruthera Wayne, the oldest of Neal and Josephine DeWitty's three children, was born on June 19th 1921 in St. Mary's Colony, Texas.

In 1940, after a romantic courtship, she married Mr. Charles Bryson Wayne, (a.k.a. "Uncle C.B.", pictured far left). In 1943 the family moved to Bremerton, WA where he worked for the Naval Shipyard.

They both joined First A.M.E. Church after settling in the Seattle, later moving to Black Diamond, WA. She served as president of the Gospel Choir while he was a member of the Senior Usher board.
Uncle C.B. was well established in the African American business community as the owner of "J and R Concrete" (Jimmie Ruthera Concrete). Aunt Jimmie (seated next to Poppee) was a supervisor for the Seattle Public Schools Food Service program for 19 years until her retirement in 1983.

My great Aunt Telitha Watson (a.k.a. "Aunt Too-Too"), the youngest of Neal and Josephine DeWitty's children, was born on February 19th 1926. She and Aunt Jimmie were avid bowlers successfully competing in tournaments.

Aunt Too-Too had a son, Don Neal Smith, born May 17th 1944. (pictured with Uncle Gordon and Auntie Bug)

Cousin Don had a "Boss" ride, a 1966 Ford Thunderbird Landau. The body was white, with a black vinyl top, and signature sequential tail lights.

(This is a photo taken in the fall of 1965 of the Lincoln/Thunderbird assembly plant in Wixom, MI)

I will always cherish my summer vacations in Black Diamond, WA with Aunt Jimmie's grandsons, Joey, Leo, and Kevin. We had great times when they came to visit from California. They are now husbands and proud fathers whom I Love very much.

"The Long Drive"

Reading Robert Frost, as we drove,
Roads aren't taken, staying Gold...
Flattening pennies, on train tracks,
Adventurous. 8 years old.

Riding Horseback, on "Old Charlie",
Loyal Doberman Pinscher, "Ben"...
My cousins, Joey, Leo, and Kevin,
Playing cards, letting me win.

I miss quiet walks to the mailbox,
Ant hills, and homemade Ice Cream...
Catching catfish at Silver Lake,
wasn't just a dream.

All Grown up, I remember,
Black Diamond, I'll Never forget...
Aunt Jimmie, Uncle C.B. send Kisses,
The Sayles Brothers and me, a Quartet.

Read Robert Frost, as we drove,
Roads not taken, stayed Gold.
Flattened pennies on train tracks,
A story still being told.

I am the daughter of Clifford R. Mollette Jr. and
Ann Ruthera DeWitty, born on August 6th 1968 at
St. Francis Cabrini Hospital in Seattle, WA.
I was named "Charron" after a family friend and
my middle name "Marie" is the same as Gram's.

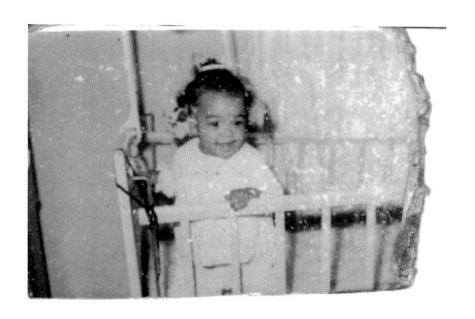

Granny captured my giggles, sniffles, and first words.

The Chinese proverb, "A journey of a thousand miles begins with one step.", means that a person must begin small achievements on his or her journey to reach their goal or destination.

Granny directed her first Short Action Film "Baby Steps" (pictured above: someone breaking in their new walking shoes). It never made it to theaters, but she cheered every stumble, bumble, and fumble.

A warm summer day with Mom as we explored the wonderment of ladybugs; pulled "weeds" (any plant growing where you don't want them); and anticipated the musical sounds of the Ice Cream truck cruising down our street.

Sitting on Granny's front steps is "Red Riding Hood" wearing the latest Spring fashion of 1971.

"Sesame Street", "The Brady Bunch", and "The Pink Panther", were just a few of the television shows loved by this 3 year old.

"Ked" sneakers were constructed for speed. I could run like a cheetah towards Granny for hugs.

"Shhh!" Don't tell anybody but...
someone,
her name rhymes with "fanny",
caught me "borrowing" her wig.

Thanks to Mom, I was "Pre-school Cool".

Shiny hardwood floors are beautiful, but turned out to be my worst nightmare. Now Mom could track my every move. The sound of hard bottom shoes could be heard from the kitchen.

"Click", I was caught sneaking into her room. Foiled once again.

My bedroom was an Art Gallery, a toy sanctuary, a music studio, and a garage for my red tricycle. It was also where Granny read to me, "The Giving Tree" by Shel Silverstein and nursed me back to health with a hot bowl of soup.

My Christmas memory. Nat King Cole's "A Christmas Song" playing in the background as we opened presents. This night gown was from Gram? Mom? Santa? I'm not really sure, I was still half asleep.

Dear Granny,

    I love you and miss you. I want to thank you for being the family photographer. You and your Brownie camera did a hell of a job. I am able to relive the special moments we shared through your photos.

Love Always,
Ron Ron

Acknowledgements

A warm-hearted Thank you to all of the people who inspired and helped me through the process of finishing this book. This project would not be possible without the support of many people.

Mr. John A. Huguley
Book Publishing & Literary Services
http://www.johnhuguley.com/

The chance encounter that changed my life. Thank you Mr. Huguley, no one has been more encouraging or supportive on this journey. This book wouldn't have been completed without your expertise and guidance.

Mr. Jack Valko
Computer Network Technician and Systems Analyst

The "Whiz Kid". Genius. Network Ninja. The Maestro. Thanks Jax.

Book Cover Photography: Ms. Ann R. DeWitty

Thanks Mom. I Love You.

Thank you to the Extraordinary Proofreading and Editing Team

In Alphabetical order by First Name:

Ms. Ann R. DeWitty
Ms. Beverly Washington
Mrs. Charlotte E. Nickles
Mr. Clifford R. Mollette Jr.
Mr. Don Neal Smith
Mr. John A. Huguley
Ms. Josephine Sayles
Mr. & Mrs. Joseph Sayles Jr.
Mr. & Mrs. Kevin Sayles
Mr. & Mrs. Leo Sayles
Ms. Shawn Franklin

Special Thanks for Photography and Images

In Alphabetical order by First Name:

Adidas (Apparel & Footwear)
Ann R. DeWitty
Auburn Valley Creative Arts Gallery
Baker City, OR (Charter Fishing)
Borracchini's Bakery
Mr. Charles McCormick
City of Hong Kong (Junkyard Boat Tours)
Courthouse Square (Tacoma, WA)
Crave Couture (Hair Studio)
David's Bridal
Epiphany School (Seattle, WA)
The Facts Newspaper (Seattle, WA)
First A.M.E. Church (Seattle, WA)
Garfield High School (Seattle, WA)
General Motors Company (Cadillac)
Girl Scouts of America
The Hawaiian Islands of Maui and O'ahu
Holy Names Academy (Seattle, WA)
JanSport Backpacks
Ked Sneakers
King Street Station (Seattle, WA)
Eastman Kodak Co. (Kodak Brownie Reflex Camera)
Lincoln/Thunderbird Assembly Plant (Wixom, MI)
The Majorettes Drill Team (Seattle, WA)
Men's Warehouse
Mercer Island Rockers Senior Softball League
Niagara Falls, NY WIBC Championship Tournament
Mr. Norman Seef
Pan-American World Airways
Polaroid Corporation (Polaroid's One-Step Camera)

(continued on next page...)

Radio Flyer (Classic Red Tricycles)
Seattle-Tacoma International Airport
Seattle City Light East Pine Substation (Central Area,
First Hill, & Capitol Hill Neighborhoods)
The Seattle Fire Department
The Seattle Post-Intelligencer
The Seattle Times Newspaper
Mr. Sly of Sly and the Family Stone
Mr. Snoop Dogg
Sparks, NV Parks and Recreation
Stacey Adams Shoe Company
Stella Louise Pettus
St. Joseph School (Seattle, WA)
Street Photographers-Seattle and Tacoma, WA
United Airlines-Seattle Softball Team
The United States Navy
University Of California, Los Angeles
The University of Washington (*Go DAWGS!!!*)
University Properties Janitorial Services
Valley Medical Center (Renton) – Birth Center
VOGUE magazine
Volkswagen (A German word meaning "People's car")
Walker Chapel A.M.E. Church (Seattle, WA)
White House Photographer
Youth Sports News-KZAM 92.5 FM
Yuen Lui Studio Photography

Loving Hugs to my Mom and Dad; my beautiful daughter Jerrelle Ann; my family; and Granny for making this journey possible.

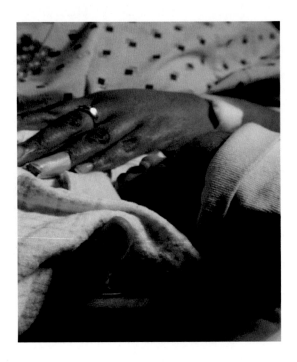

My Precious Jerrelle,

You are my Inspiration. My Masterpiece. I miss you Every day and Love you more than Life itself.

Love Always,
Mommy

(Hair Styled by Ms. Candace of "Crave Couture")

About the Author

Published Author Charron M. Mollette of the book "Pen and Paper" is a native of Seattle, Washington. Her previous work was included in the book "Under the Harvest Moon" where she received the "Editor's Choice Award" from the National Library of Poetry. A huge fan of Shel Silverstein and Robert Frost, she also enjoys Art Galleries.